Senses

The Sixth Sense
and Other Special Senses

Karen Hartley, Chris Macro and Philip Taylor

Heinemann
LIBRARY

First published in Great Britain by Heinemann Library,
Halley Court, Jordan Hill, Oxford OX2 8EJ
a division of Reed Educational and Professional Publishing Ltd.
Heinemann is a registered trademark of Reed Educational & Professional Publishing Ltd.

OXFORD MELBOURNE AUCKLAND
JOHANNESBURG BLANTYRE GABORONE
IBADAN PORTSMOUTH (NH) USA CHICAGO

© Reed Educational and Professional Publishing Ltd 2001
The moral right of the proprietor has been asserted.

Designed by Celia Floyd
Illustrated by Alan Fraser
Originated by Ambassador Litho Ltd, UK
Printed in Hong Kong / China

05 04 03 02 01
10 9 8 7 6 5 4 3 2 1

ISBN 0 431 09732 1
This title is also available in a hardback library edition (ISBN 0 431 09725 9).

British Library Cataloguing in Publication Data

Hartley, Karen
  The sixth sense and other special senses. – (Senses)
  1. Senses and sensation – Juvenile literature
  2. Intuition – Juvenile literature
  I. Title II. Macro, Chris III. Taylor, Philip
  573.8'7

Acknowledgements

The Publishers would like to thank the following for permission to reproduce photographs:

Bruce Coleman: Erwin & Peggy Bouer p.28, Kim Taylor p.19; Corbis: Joe McDonald p.29; Heather Angel p.18; Heinemann: Gareth Boden p.4, p.5, p.7, p.8, p.9, p.15, p.24, p.26, p.27; John Walmsley p.13, p.14; Oxford Scientific Films: Anna Walsh p.25, Daniel J Cox p.23, GI Bernard p.20, John Downer p.22; Pictor International p.6, p.10, p.12, p.17; Tony Stone: Art Wolfe p.16, Jeff Rotman p.21, John Warden p.11.

Cover photograph reproduced with permission of Oxford Scientific Films and Gareth Boden.

Many thanks to the teachers and pupils of Abbotsweld Primary School, Harlow.

Every effort has been made to contact copyright holders of any material reproduced in this book. Any omissions will be rectified in subsequent printings if notice is given to the Publisher.

For more information about Heinemann Library books, or to order, please telephone +44 (0)1865 888066, or send a fax to +44 (0)1865 314091. You can visit our web site at www.heinemann.co.uk

Any words appearing in the text in bold, **like this**, are explained in the Glossary.

Contents

What are your senses?

People and animals have senses to help them find out about the world. You use your senses to feel, see, hear, taste and smell. Your senses can warn you of danger.

You use your ears to hear, your eyes to see and your tongue to taste. You use your skin to touch. There are other special senses which work inside your body.

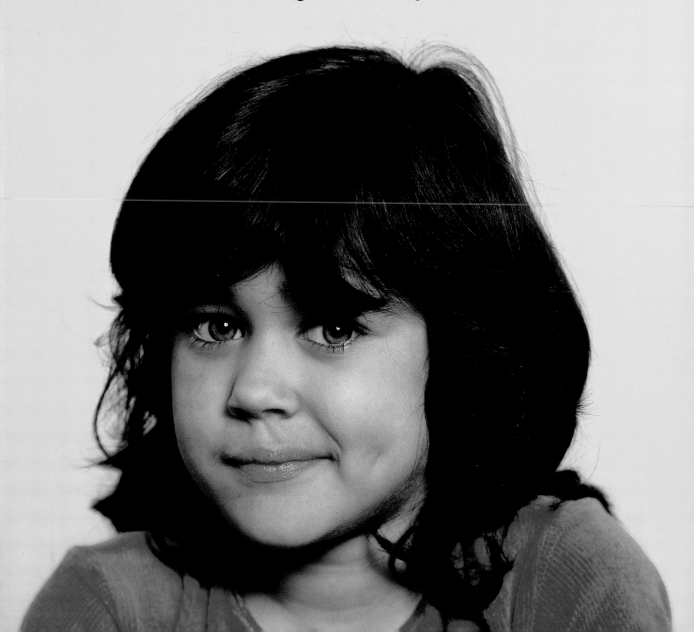

What are the special senses?

People and animals have special senses. These special senses work inside your body. The inside senses tell you when you are hungry, thirsty, sleepy or in pain.

People have a sense of **rhythm**. You also have a sense of **balance** which stops you falling over and helps you when you walk on walls or on the benches in school.

Why do you feel hungry?

If you have not got enough sugar in your blood you feel very hungry. When you eat, the feeling of hunger goes away.

Your brain has special parts which tell you how much water is in your body. If there is not enough, you feel thirsty. If there is too much, then you need to go to the toilet.

What is rhythm?

When you dance, you move your legs and feet in a pattern. Often this is in time to some music. When you clap or beat a drum you are moving your hands in a pattern.

Some people have a very good sense of **rhythm**. This means that they can feel the patterns in their bodies when they stamp or clap. Can you clap a pattern of sounds?

What is balance?

When you climb in a playground, you use your sense of **balance**. This stops you from falling over and hurting yourself. Many parts of your body help your sense of balance.

There is a liquid in your ear which helps you to keep your balance. Your eyes and your **muscles** also help you to keep your balance.

Animals' special senses

Many animals' senses are much better than yours. Dogs can smell things which you cannot smell. Bats can hear things which you cannot hear. Dolphins can see in very deep water where it is very dark.

Some animals have senses which help them to feel the heat from other animals. Other animals such as jellyfish can sense light, sound and movement through their skin.

Changing colour

Some flatfish can change their colour so that they cannot be seen on the bottom of the sea. Do you think that this flatfish can be seen by its enemies?

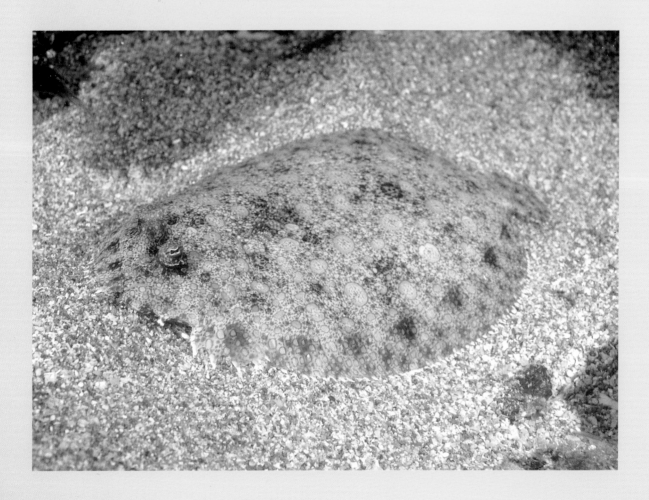

The **chameleon** changes colour when the light gets brighter or darker and when it is frightened. Its special senses tell it when to change colour.

Using special senses

Animals have special senses which help them to keep safe and to find food. The cockroach has a **vibration feeler** in its leg. It can tell when other animals or people are near.

Sharks eat **injured** animals in the sea. They can smell a tiny drop of blood far away. They also feel the **electricity** in the bodies of the fish that they are going to eat.

Finding the way home

Some birds have a sort of **compass** inside them which helps them to find their way. Pigeons use the sun and the stars to help them to find their way home.

Salmon have a special sense which helps them to find their way home. People think that the salmon can tell from the **scents** it smells in the water which way to go.

Plant senses

Plants use their senses to find the light. Plants need light to grow. Can you see how this plant has become bent because it is trying to grow towards the light?

Some plants eat insects. When the **bladderwort** feels an insect on its special hairs, it sucks the insect into its trap.

The 'sixth sense'

Some people say that you have a sixth sense. Some people can tell if there is another person standing behind them, even if they cannot hear them or see them.

Sometimes pets have this sixth sense too. It is called an **instinct**. They can tell when their owners are coming home, even when they cannot see them.

Investigating special senses

This girl is blindfolded. Another child has tiptoed silently into the room. Do you think that the **blindfolded** girl will know that someone is there?

Some people say that the sixth sense can tell us what is going to happen next. Do you think that these children can tell what card is going to be turned over next?

Did you know?

Some snakes such as the **pit viper** have special heat **feelers** inside their heads. They can feel the heat from the bodies of the animals which they are hunting to eat.

Did you know that a **duckbilled platypus** can tell if an **electric** battery is nearby?

Did you know that some animals have a sense which tells them when to go to sleep for the winter?

Glossary

balance   an inside sense which keeps you from falling over

bladderwort   a plant which grows in water and eats little insects

blindfolded   when something is tied over your eyes so you cannot see

chameleon   an animal which looks like a lizard and can change colour

compass   a small, round object with a magnetic pointer inside. People use a compass to help them find their way.

electricity   invisible energy

feelers   thin growths from the heads of some animals which help them to know what is around them

duckbilled platypus   an animal with four legs and a beak like a duck

injured   when a person or an animal is hurt

instinct   a feeling which you cannot explain

muscles   parts of the body which make the person or animal move

pit viper   a snake

receivers   parts of the bodies of animals and people, which send messages from your body to your brain

rhythm   a feeling in your body which helps you to feel and hear the patterns in music

salmon   a fish

scents   another word for smells

vibration   a shaking movement

Sense map

How do bats find their food?

sounds come from the bat's mouth and bounce off the insect

echoes which go into the bats ears

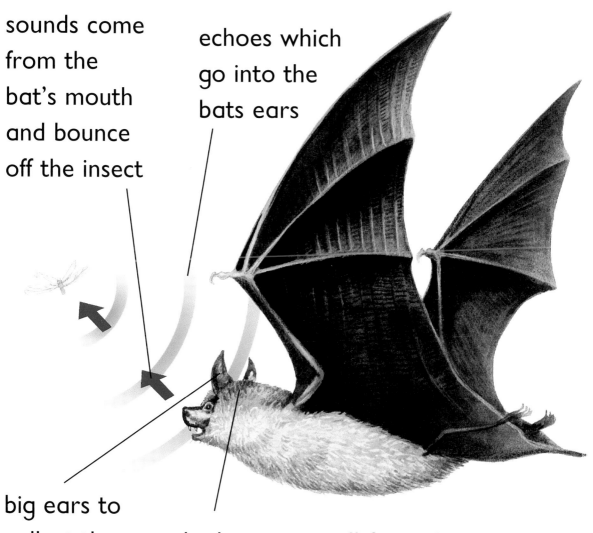

big ears to collect the echo sounds

the brain can tell from the echoes exactly where the insect is

Index